Stars
and
Firelight

Books by the Authors

Stars
and
Firelight

Gladis & Gordon DePree

Illustrations by Martha Bentley

ZONDERVAN
PUBLISHING HOUSE
OF THE ZONDERVAN CORPORATION
GRAND RAPIDS, MICHIGAN 49506

Stars and Firelight
Copyright © 1981 by The Zondervan Corporation

This printing August 1981

Library of Congress Cataloging in Publication Data

DePree, Gladis, 1933-
    Stars & Firelight.

    1. Meditations.   I. DePree, Gordon.   II. Title.
III. Title: Stars and firelight.
BV4832.2.D4488   242'.5   81-11450
ISBN 0-310-44121-8   AACR2

Scripture passages are from the Jerusalem Bible, copyright
1966 by Barton, Longman & Todd, Ltd. and Doubleday &
Company, Inc.

Edited by Mary Bombara
Design by Mary Bombara and Martha Bentley

Printed in the United States of America

Perhaps they are the same essential fire—but one is distant, dazzling, always out beyond our grasp, while the other is close, warm, and congenial. We need them both, the challenge and the comfort, the wonder and the warmth, the span of the Universe and the security of home. We need both

STARS AND FIRELIGHT

"I have this complaint to make; you have less love than you used to. Think where you were before you fell."
Revelation 2:4–5

1

LIFE IS A progression—a series of insights gained, lived out, outgrown, then reborn in new ideas which again start the whole cycle. As a person I hope to grow in understanding and wisdom.

But in the search for knowing more, there may come moments of nostalgia. Picking up an old letter, looking through diaries or old pictures with all the memories they recreate. . . . The thought may flash across my mind, *Was there a time when I loved more than I do?*

Was there a time when my life was more people-centered, when I wanted less and gave more? Was there a time when my love for God was less double-minded? To grow in understanding is a great goal, but it is only worth pursuing if my *love* of life and God can grow in proportion to all else gained.

"If what was so temporary had any splendor, there must be much more in what is going to last forever. Now this Lord is the Spirit, and where the Spirit of the Lord is, there is freedom."
2 Corinthians 3:11, 18

WHAT A TUG OF war! I find myself torn between two needs in life, permanence and freedom. Part of me wants to settle into a big family home with a fireplace and homebaked bread and scores of friends and children, and part of me wants to go backpacking in Tibet.

How can one find a life that is permanent yet does not ossify into a deadly rut? What is both stable and moveable, new and lasting? What fires the imagination, yet gives a sense of continuity?

Knowing the presence of the Spirit of God can give us both of these seemingly irreconcilable extremes. When we live *in God* we can be always on a journey and always at home.

". . . a lamp in my presence."
1 Kings 11:36

3

THERE IS A WARM quality about the glow of
lamplight or the flicker of a candle flame that
soothes and relaxes. After seeing the bright
lights of the city, flashing and glaring,
advertising and enticing, it is peaceful to sit
down and gaze into the light of a solitary
candle flame, to feel its soft glow bathing
one's face in gentle warmth. There is no
harshness, no insistence in a candle
flame . . . instead, it coaxes one to be quiet,
to reflect, to come out of hiding within
oneself and commune with greatness.

I would like to live as a candle flame in my
relationships with other people; not forcing
ideas on them, but being a soft glow that
puts them in the best light, and helps them to
get in touch with themselves. I would like to
gently soothe, and make those who share my
life feel that they have been in the presence
of the God who lives in me—and in them.

*"This is the way you ought to talk,
neighbor to neighbor, brother to
brother, 'What answer has Yahweh
given?' or 'What has Yahweh said?'"*
Jeremiah 23:35

4

I WOULD RATHER be a communicator than a
pronouncer. Pronouncers stand on their high
and holy pedestals and let the word drop;
communicators sit on the floor or around a
table and dig into each other's hearts and
minds.

The communication of our faith scares many
of us. We see it as a situation in which we,
the holy, face a hostile and basically ungodly
world. If this is our attitude, we should be
afraid! But if we can see each neighbor as
someone God loves, someone who is living a
life that, even though it is being expressed
differently than ours, is still valuable in God's
sight . . . if we can see our neighbors as
fellow humans with whom we love to share a
person-to-person chat, we will begin to better
understand the love of God ourselves. And
in that larger understanding, we may find
that the person next door has as much to
teach us as we have to teach him or her.
Communication is a two-way street.
Pronouncement pedestals are lonely places.

"As for Mary, she treasured all these things and pondered them in her heart."
Luke 2:19

CHRISTMAS IS A time for treasuring and pondering. It is a season of beloved old customs . . . carols that we have heard over and over, familiar family recipes, the little crèche and the wreath on the door. Christmas is not a time for innovating. We want to bring out our old treasures, to take a loving look at them and be affirmed.

But the old and the new are bound up together. Each year when we take out our treasured decorations, we ourselves are not the same as we were last year. We will have passed through new areas, new perceptions, hopefully have gained some new wisdom; and the eyes through which we view the old treasures will be slightly different. What the changes are, it is hard to say, for life deepens and widens almost imperceptibly. Each year the old treasures suggest a new dimension of love and faith, sometimes too profound to be verbalized. Perhaps it is best if, like Mary, we treasure all these things and ponder them in our hearts.

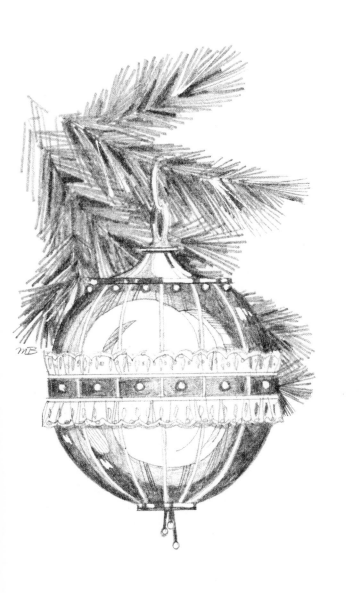

*"If you . . . follow my commandments
. . . I will make my home among
[you]."*
1 Kings 6:12

MANY OF US WISH to have the presence of God felt in our homes. We hang up posters or plaques or scripture portions or other meaningful reminders. But as useful as these are, they will not tempt God into our walls.

The home where God's presence is felt is one where a few simple rules are kept. These rules can be summed up in the words, "You shall love the Lord your God with all your heart . . . and your neighbor as yourself." They are old, old words, and we may sometimes grow tired of hearing them, but they contain all the sense of awe, all the deep respect that is needed to give our lives a sense of worth and our relationships a firm base. Like so many of the promises in the Bible, this is more than a sugared carrot held out to make us behave. It is a set of conditions which will bring about a natural result. If we honestly love God, others, and even ourselves, we will find that we are living where God is very much at home.

*"Were he to pass me, I should not see
him, nor detect his stealthy
movement."*
Job 9:11

?

WHEN THE DIRECTION of my life is unclear and
days pass along with a sense of inner
emptiness, I wish I could be in touch with
God, could have some visible proof that he is
there. But all I can see is the parade of
events: morning, noon, and night—life
events like sleeping and waking, eating and
working. Things come and go, and where is
God?

And then I understand that God is like the
giant shadow, the silent presence in all
things, never standing outside life, but living
in the sleeping and waking, the eating and
working. His presence is the stealthy
movement within all things. He has been
there all along. . . . All that must become
clearer is my eye to see him. I so quickly
forget that God lives in the ordinary as well
as in the spectacular.

"The prophet who prophesies peace can only be recognized as one truly sent by Yahweh when his word comes true."
Jeremiah 28:9

8

MANY OF US TALK about peace. Politicians win elections by talking about international peace. Christmas is the most popular festival in the Western world because it enshrines the idea of "peace on earth." Leaders become popular when they find ways to assure people of peace in their souls. . . .

But when the individual encounters the issue of peace or non-peace within, there is no room for rhetoric or posturing. The fact is faced squarely. Am I at peace with myself? Am I in touch with the source of my being? Are the words of peace I speak real? This is where the truth lies.

"Finally, brothers, fill your minds with everything that is true . . . noble . . . good . . . pure, everything that we love and honor, and everything that can be thought virtuous or worthy of praise. . . . Then the God of peace will be with you."

Philippians 4:8, 9

9

IT IS A SIMPLE equation of the mind and spirit. If I fill my mind with truth, goodness, love, honor, and whatever is highest in life, my spirit will be at peace with God.

But frankly, I am not always at peace. I cast about, trying to choose between this aspect of truth and that. Being noble is hard when I'd rather get even, and thinking about God's goodness is embarrassing when I need one thing more. Being motivated by love and honor is a high road, and sometimes I choose the low road and am motivated by selfishness and greed instead. Being virtuous and giving praise seem a little duller than being savvy and cynical. And the strange thing is I'm free to do as I like, but then I must pay the price. When I make troubling choices, my heart will not have the peace of God.

"If you are wise, study these things and realize how Yahweh shows his love."
Psalm 107:43

10

WHEN A BOAT is caught in a storm at sea, the sailors will never live to give thanks unless they do their best to get to shore. In times of drought, cities build new waterworks so they can retain the rain when it falls. No one ever had a harvest to thank God for without planting the seed, and no one ever had a family to be thankful for without going through the hard work and deep soul-searching required to maintain it.

There are many things that we give thanks for, because we know that in spite of all our efforts it is still God who sends the rain and creates life. But we cannot expect God to work miracles in our lives unless we have been sufficiently involved in the solution of our own problems to recognize a miracle when we see one.

"Let me . . . take pride in being one of your heirs."
Psalm 106:5

11

THE TERM "child of God" has many different meanings to different people. To some it is a state they have become conscious of lately, to others it means being a child of the universe, with as much right to belong as the stars.

However I have come to this awareness, what does it *mean* to me, to be a child of God? To me it means that all God is, I am heir to. All that God does, I participate in. The whole wonderful and terrible range of God's responsibilities to his creation are also, in a smaller way, my responsibilities. The sense of balance between justice and mercy, the ability to know and understand the worst there is to know, and to still go on loving the world and its people. . . . The eternal struggle between light and darkness, between dying to old things and living to new horizons. . . . All these become my lot as a child of God.

It is a birthright to be used with reverence and awe.

"Yes, God loved the world so much that he gave. . . ."
John 3:16

12

HOW MANY MOTIVATIONS we have for the giving of gifts! Mrs. Jones gave us a gift last year, so we really *should* . . . and it would be good for the business if we gave something to Mr. Smith . . . and Mrs. Brown is a good contact, we *should* remember her . . . and where is the list of people we got cards from last year?

Should? Christmas is a time when, once a year, we have a chance to purify our hearts and think through the meaning of giving. *God loved the world so much that he gave. . . .* That is what Christmas is all about—loving and giving. It is a box of cookies baked with love and given to someone who will do us no earthly good. It is spontaneity, and a warm tear when we sing "Silent Night, Holy Night." Loving is the only excuse for giving. . . . If there is someone we *should* give a gift to this Christmas, maybe we *shouldn't.*

"I mean to sing to Yahweh all my life."
Psalm 104:33

13

THE INTENTION, the direction, the overarching meaning of my life is what will be important in the long run. The true intention of my spirit will win out over seeming lapses of that intent.

I mean to be in a creative frame of mind all my life, but occasionally circumstances pile up and I find myself on the edge of panic. Despair, doubt, cynicism—all the destructive emotions wash over me, nearly drowning me. But there is no genuine cause for fear, as long as the intention of my heart is to praise and create, and to be in touch with God. What I intend to do, I will do. Life will pop up again, like a ball held under water.
I intend to sing. I will sing.

". . . the tongue is a flame . . ."
James 3:6

14

A FLAME CAN be either a negative or positive thing. It depends on what use I put the fire to, whether I use it to burn or bless, to warm or wound.

Words spoken in anger, in desperation, or even in self-defense, can inflict a deep burn. No matter how much we may wish to retrieve them, the healing may take a long painful process and may leave scars on the spirit. On the other hand, words spoken in love, in caring, words expressing confidence in another person, can bring warmth and glow to a spirit. Words that say, *"I respect you as a valid human being, I want to stand by you while you grow, I believe there is something good in you, I think you are beautiful. . . ."* Such warm words not only affirm us, but bring out in us qualities that we never dreamed existed.

The tongue is a flame. God, help me to use my flame to warm, and not to scorch, the earth.

" 'I have neither silver nor gold, but I will give you what I have.' . . . Peter then took him by the hand and helped him to stand up."
Acts 3:6–7

15

THE SIGHT OF the Christmas tree, shining and festive is an exciting part of the holidays. When it is up and the sound of carols rings through the house, we begin to feel the old magic happening again. . . .

But some of the best gifts we can give each other this year will not be put under the tree. They cannot be bought or sold or wrapped or, perhaps, even premeditated. They certainly cannot be shopped for. If we don't have them in the house already, we can't give them.

In our celebrations as a family and with friends the most significant giving takes place when we reach out to each other and say, "More than any material gift, I give you the gift of my love. I share with you my faith, I care about your life. . . . Have courage. Your life is also a gift that has been given to the world. Celebrate it!"

To give these gifts is a true celebration of Christ.

*"Whether we like it or not, we mean
to obey the voice of Yahweh our
God . . . and by thus obeying . . . we
will prosper."*
Jeremiah 42:6

16

THAT TINY PROMPTING that catches me off
guard in the middle of the night or comes
into my mind while walking down the
street . . . could it be the voice of God,
whispering over the darkness and busyness
of my life . . . telling me to forgive what I find
unforgivable, to love what I feel is unlovable,
to open myself to newness of heart?

Whatever that voice is, if I brush it aside I will
know a terrible emptiness and a sense of
failure; but if I listen to it and follow it,
whether I like it or not, some kind of healing
can begin.

I hear it, deeper and more penetrating than
all other sounds. What does it say? In my
response to that wordless whisper is the key
to my own wholeness.

"Love no flood can quench, no torrents drown."
Song of Songs 8:7

17

LOVE IS THE glowing fire burning in the heart of each living being. With it, we reach out and touch each other. We are sustained by the glow of this life force that flows between us, this eternal fire of God within us.

When the storms of self-doubt threaten to blow out the glow, we turn to one another to relight our fires. When the rains of aloneness pour down and all but extinguish our flame, we seek one another to give that sputtering flame new courage. The love of others lights our darkness, and refuses to let us be put out . . . usually. . . .

But when it happens that our darkness is complete, and no other light will revive us, we have only to turn to the great glowing source of love and light. One touch, and our love-light is rekindled.

"I have treasured your promises in my heart, since I have no wish to sin against you."
Psalm 119:11

18

BEING "RIGHT WITH God" is an old-fashioned term that has great religious and even psychological significance. If I am angry at God, if I feel the basic scheme of the universe is unfair and unjust, this anger breaks out in a thousand forms . . . from arrogance and narcissism to belligerence toward others.

But if I accept the world and its Creator, the flow of events and the ultimate power as being good and right, I find I have no need to strike back. The goodness of God becomes life's greatest fascination, and evil is seen as destructive, rather than as the natural order of things. If I have no *wish* to strike back at God, I will hurt myself and others much less.

*"And these in turn were to tell it to
their own children so that they too
would put their confidence in God . . .
not becoming like their ancestors
. . . in spirit unfaithful to God."*
Psalm 78:7–8

19

TRADITIONS COME to us from a past where
people were caught in the complexities of life
and struggled to lay down some format that
would help them cope with their realities.
They did not come from a rosy past where
the old boys did it all right.

When we pass traditions on to our children,
we know that we are giving them the
ambiguities of the past. It is like handing
them a firebrand with the words, "Here, this
has never completely illuminated the
darkness before you, but it is better than no
light at all." And when we know we have
shared what we can, we leave the future up
to them. Each generation's hope that they
will make the future better keeps the human
race reaching toward God.

"I knew you then only by hearsay; but now . . . with my own eyes."
Job 42:5

Much of what we "know" has come to us through the experience of others. We read, we listen, we learn by observing. . . . Yet no matter how large this store of knowledge is, we do not deeply understand anything until we have experienced it personally.

We can always say, "I care," but to say to a person going through a serious illness, "I understand," is simply not true unless we too have been there. To try to understand a deep rift or heartache between parents and children is difficult unless we have wept the same kind of bitter tears. To speak to anyone at a time of death or accident or divorce is only *words,* unless these experiences have also touched our lives at close range. It seems ironic that all of the things we strive most earnestly to avoid in life are the very experiences that make us more authentic channels of God's love. Perhaps it is not our own goodness that is on the line, but our ability to communicate the power and healing love of God.

"My Strength, I play for you. . . ."
Psalm 59:17

21

ALTHOUGH FEW OF US are going to startle the world with our musical ability, we can think of ourselves as being in concert with God.

As we awake each morning, the pulsing music of the universe is ringing through space. All around us there is a song of gladness and power and joy and strength. But sometimes the voice of this song is very quiet, and is almost shouted down by other voices . . . sadness and weakness and despair. Yet if we can catch the melody of that ringing love song and begin to play the strings of our lives to accompany it, it grows clearer in the spot of the earth where we stand. We can be God's accompanists, making his voice stronger in this world.

"And she gave birth to a son, her firstborn. . . . and laid him in a manger."
Luke 2:6–7

WHAT IS IT THAT inspires us so deeply at the Christmas season of each year . . . that tugs at us and makes us our best?

Christmas, in the birth of Christ, brings us face to face with our basic humanity. It brings us to straw, and sheep, and shepherds, and a young mother in the pangs of her first childbirth. It is the warm breath of cows, and a barn, and bright starlight on a cold night.

It is all of these, and yet it is something more. It is angel songs and mystery, and unexpected visitors who declare the newborn to be royal. It is a miracle, brought about in the context of ordinary things; it is a baby's cry, echoed by a heavenly host. It starts with the common and lifts us into a sense of awe so gently that we do not know how we have been transported. But one thing we do know: ever since that first Christmas we have understood what it means for God to dwell with us. Our common lives have been given a dimension of holiness.

23

THE KIND OF FREEDOM Jesus Christ gives us is a great relief. He frees us from the bondage of old thoughts and gives us new images. He frees us from old values and gives us new motivations. He frees us from being the center of our own world and gives us love for every other person who lives. He makes our scope bigger and brighter and deeper and stronger, until we feel so free we could shout for joy!

I know this—except for the times when I slip back into the old bondage, and become stereotyped and possessed by things, and centered on myself, claiming I have a *right* to do so. But once I have exercised these rights I know they are not right for me at all, and that all I want is to let go and be filled again with so much freedom and light that the darkness can no longer contain me.

"You have made him a little less than a god."
Psalm 8:5

24

WE ARE CREATIONS of God, with a loose connection to the power source. One moment we are glowing with power, and the next we are dead, lifeless, and limp. We are made in God's likeness, but sometimes the light dims in our eye.

A little less than a god. . . . Gods are always right. They make decisions and never have to change them. Their edicts stand forever. We are *quite a bit* less than gods . . . so right one moment and the next moment stung with the smallness of our minds, the sea of things we have not comprehended. God has made us a little less than gods in our own right. We still need the source.

*". . . actually destroying in his own
person the hostility caused by the rules
and decrees of the Law. . . . In his
own person he killed the hostility."*
Ephesians 2:14–15, 17

I MAY BE ANGRY at you, and you at me, and we
both may have good reasons. But if both of
us can prove that we are right, how can we
ever agree?

It is hard to answer this question until one
thinks of a life like Christ's. His was a life that
took an abrupt turn in a different direction, a
life with meaning so refreshing, so
all-encompassing, so startling in its simplicity,
that both sides of an argument were left
speechless. He was a person whose
greatness made people recognize petty
arguments for the trivia that they were.

In the small scope of my life, I would like to
be that kind of person . . . always reaching
for the larger and the truer to neutralize the
lesser and the questionable.

"Nothing will bring relief but speech."
Job 32:20

VERBALIZING A concern makes it more possible to cope with it. Call this the need to ventilate, to let it all out, or whatever you will, but the opportunity to have a good talk with a trusted friend is a great release.

Most of the time we have someone we can share concerns with, but sometimes we are left alone. What we have to share might cause more harm than good, and we sit in our aloneness, building up resentment like a poison. . . . What can be done?

There is never a concern that we cannot talk over with God. The honest outpouring of a seeking heart before God is a very healing thing . . . and if we listen carefully to what we say to God, we may even find the key to the solution of our own problems.

"Happy the man [or woman] . . ."
Psalm 112:1

27

HAPPY THE MAN (or woman) whose life is filled
with the love of God. Happy the man who
joyfully keeps God's commandments. He is a
man who shines like a mellow lamp in a dark
night. He is merciful, he has a tender heart,
he is not ashamed to be good. He is honest,
even when it doesn't pay. He is steadfast to
the point of stubbornness, even-tempered,
trusts in God even when he doesn't have
much to go on, never loses his head even at
the worst news. He can admit and overcome
his fears, be generous with what he has, and
realistic in his relationships with others.

And happy the woman who shares such a
man's life.

*"Bear with one another, forgive each
other as soon as a quarrel begins.
Always be thankful."*
Colossians 3:13, 15

THERE ARE SOME roads we travel down which,
as soon as we start them, the sign WRONG
WAY flashes up in bright red. The road of
being angry with each other, of losing
tempers, of dumping latent hostility on each
other, of saying cutting things. . . . The only
thing to do is to turn around and get off the
road, or there will be a collision.

But there are other roads we can travel on
forever and, even without any road signs to
reassure us, know that we are headed the
right way. The road of being thankful for
each other's lives, for our own lives, for work
to do, and love to share, for all of life's good
gifts. . . . This is the way. Being on the right
road is the only way to get where we want
to go.

"For Yahweh is creating something new on earth."
Jeremiah 31:22

THE WORLD AND ITS creatures were created in the beginning, and in the minds of some of us, it has been downhill ever since. In the minds of others, the human race climbs an inch each year in the long struggle toward realizing what it was that we were created to be.

Right or wrong, I prefer to live by the second mindset. If I can believe that some of the best ideas are yet to be discovered, that much of the greatest music is yet to be heard, that many of the greatest books are yet to be written, some of the most profound pictures yet to be painted, and some of the greatest men and women yet to be born, I can live my one small life in a sense of expectant forward motion. I do believe that God, the great power, is still creating something new on this earth.

"For Yahweh has been kind to his people, conferring victory on us who are weak."
Psalm 149:4

30

IT IS EASY TO lose sight of our overarching goals as we live from day to day. Lost in the winding maze of our daily existence, everything falls a little short—dreams with just a few flaws in them, weather that is too hot or too cold, letters that seem to take years to come, things to be done that we really don't want to do, money too quickly spent with too little to show for it, vast stretches of the day that slip by while the list of things to be accomplished goes undiminished. . . .

And then a year passes, and we look back. Somehow, miraculously, goals have been reached, projects completed, adventures lived. How did we, weak and disorganized, do so much? God was kind, conferring victory on us who were weak, because under the confusion, there was the *will* to create, to be strong.

*"Explain to me how to respect your
Law and how to observe it
wholeheartedly."*
Psalm 119:34

31

WE NEVER understand anything until we
discover it ourselves . . . usually the hard
way.

A young person may be given a rule, and
never understand why the rule was made
until he or she breaks it. The rule may be
broken with no result . . . for a while; and
then one day the understanding comes, in a
rush of hurt and remorse. But until that
stinging *why* is realized, the rule seemed
senseless.

It would be good if God could teach us
without letting us make mistakes, wouldn't it?
That is one of those yes–no questions.
Sometimes our mistakes teach us more than
our goodness, for when we understand *why*,
we can follow God from the heart.
Wholeheartedly.

"I have learnt to manage on whatever I have, I know how to be poor and I know how to be rich. . . . I am ready for anything anywhere. . . . poverty or plenty."
Philippians 4:11–12

32

PAUL HAD A PURPOSE in life, and the accomplishment of that purpose was his all-consuming goal. How much or how little he had was beside the point.

When we have a goal in life, *things* are always seen as secondary, never primary. We see times when money is scarce as a challenge to the imagination, and times when money is more plentiful as a test of the spirit, to use wisely what is ours without letting it distract or distort our values. The secret of staying steady through all of life's plenty and poverty is to know that what one *is,* what one is *doing,* and where one is *going* are all so much more important than what one *has.* Things are only the containers of purposes, and have no meaning in themselves. The purpose is what matters.

"We prove we are God's servants by our purity, knowledge, patience and kindness; by a spirit of holiness, by a love free from affectation."
2 Corinthians 6:6

IF I WANT TO live as a channel of creation in this world, I must want to be a single-minded conduit of God's creating power. What I know, I will know from the heart, and that knowledge will stem from love. I will be patient, sensing time as God sees it, viewing myself and others as slowly growing into what we are not yet. The knowing and the patience will give me a sense of kindliness; and my reverence for God will express itself in a respect for people created in his image. In this attitude, all of life will take on an aura of holiness, even in the dark moments.

And in this heart-knowing and patience and kindliness and reverence for God and life, there will grow such a love that I will never have to pretend. I will genuinely *be* a loving, creative person.

"If they sin against you—for there is no man who does not sin—and . . . if they turn again to you with all their heart and soul . . . forgive your people . . . for they are your people."
1 Kings 8:46, 48, 50–51

34

Two SETS OF expectations toward life can be adopted. One is that a low level is a human being's natural state, that we cannot expect very much of ourselves, and that occasionally, almost by default, we can accomplish something good. The other attitude is that goodness, productivity, creativity, beauty and joy are our right, and that anything less than these is a slip, a desecration of the life that lives within us.

As a follower of Jesus Christ, I choose to think of the higher plane as the natural one, allowing for the fact that I will often fail to measure up to it. At least in this context the slips will be the exception, not the rule.

"It is for this I struggle wearily on, helped only by his power driving me irresistibly."
Colossians 1:29

35

EVERY LIFE THAT IS filled with health and energy is driven in some direction. Drive is a deep urging, a call within to press out and on, to attain some goal. Having drive in life is the opposite of apathy and deadness.

But the worth of my life as seen woven into the whole pattern of other lives will not be measured by how much drive I have, but by what I am driven to do. What are my inner compulsions? What triggers them? Where am I being driven? If I think of myself as a container of the power of God, these are questions I will want to ask, thoughtfully.

"When Solomon grew old, his wives swayed his heart to other gods; and his heart was not wholly with Yahweh his God."
1 Kings 11:4

36

LOVE FOR ALL PEOPLE, tolerance, openmindedness, a curious mind and a seeking heart . . . all of these are means to becoming a wiser human being. These take a person ranging far and wide into other cultures and lifestyles, and are the mark of a knowledgeable and sophisticated man or woman.

Yet in order to maintain one's inner identity, the heart and the mind can be regarded separately in the matter of beliefs. In my mind, I can agree that every form of worship has its validity to the worshiper, that each is a genuine reaching out of the spirit of man to the creative source as it is understood. But while I know this in my mind, in my heart I must have a loving tie to one form of belief, or I will become a spiritual wanderer. Worship is an instinct in humans, but unless I personally know deeply *what* and in *whom* I believe, I will always be an outsider to the whole scene, looking on wistfully.

"You have learnt by now what the kings of Assyria have done. . . . Are you likely to be spared? What power to help did the gods have of those nations that my fathers destroyed?"
2 Kings 19:11–12

37

FAITH IS OF VERY little use unless it is strong enough to stand by us in life's extreme moments. When deep disappointments come, when sickness must be endured, when financial reverses occur or I must face the death of a friend . . . what reason do I have to feel that I will be spared devastation and despondency?

I have reason, if I know in whom I have faith. When the object of my faith is the fulfillment of wishes, or perfect health, or riches, or even the perpetual continuation of a life on this earth—when these are my gods—I will not be spared. But when the object of my faith is God, the source of life both now and forever, there is no way I can be utterly defeated. And when the hard question comes, *"Are you likely to be spared?"* the answer is *"Yes, if I keep clear my idea of who is God."*

"So give encouragement to each other, and keep strengthening one another."
1 Thessalonians 5:11

38

LIFE WITHIN A family or a friendship is a constant seesaw. Today I'm up and you're down, tomorrow you're up and I'm down. The one who is strong and up needs to be caring and loving toward the one who is weak and down.

When I'm feeling on top of the world, it is easy for me to be impatient with people who are having a rough day. I may inwardly feel superior to them and subtly add even more pain to their depression. And if I do so, I will only engender in them the kind of hostility that will make them glad to see me tumble. But if I surround friends or family members with love and caring when things look black, they may return the favor when I need it most. Remember, on any kind of a seesaw, it's the one who is down who has both feet on the ground. The one who is up is in the precarious position.

"Do not speak harshly to a man older than yourself, but advise him as you would your own father; treat younger men as brothers and older women as you would your mother. Always treat young women . . . as if they were sisters."

1 Timothy 5:1–2

39

IF EVERY OLDER man or woman I meet, of any race, can be seen as my mother or father, how differently I will look at them! I will have a respect for the life they have lived. I will be interested in them, concerned for their feelings, and my attitude will be warm and loving. My words will be kind, my looks reassuring, and I will have patience.

If every younger person I meet can be seen as my sister or brother, or son or daughter, days can be full of interpersonal relationships of deepest meaning. My questions will be asked with understanding, my reactions will be soothing, not scathing. I think I understand what Jesus meant when he looked down from the cross and said, "Mother behold your son," and "son, behold your mother." He was saying, "Behold the world, my family."

"Let all my enemies, discredited . . .
fall back in utter confusion."
Psalm 6:10

40

WHEN PEOPLE become my enemies, I can usually count on the fact that they are doing something I would hate myself for if I were doing it to them. But on the other hand I've come to dislike them so much, I could almost do it if I had a chance. It is like a hate merry-go-round.

No, it is useless and immature to hate people or to consider them my enemies, no matter what they have done. They are not for me to judge and their actions are their own responsibility. My real enemies cannot be people. They are things called despair, discouragement, muddled thinking, lack of motivation, inability to adjust to the world as I find it, disillusionment and confusion of purpose. If I could conquer all these enemies within myself, I would find far less to blame on other people.

*"Each man that stands on the earth is
only a puff of wind . . . a shadow . . . a
guest . . . a nomad."*
Psalm 39:4, 5, 12

41

PERHAPS VIEWED from the perspective of all
eternity, my life does not look like much.
I may be frail, a shadow, a puff of wind, a
guest, and a nomad. . . .

But while I am alive, I refuse to see myself in
such shadowy terms. I may be frail, but I am
a part of what is strong. My small puff of
wind has in it the breath of God; my shadow
is cast by being near the Light; I am a guest
of the Almighty, and a nomad in search of
beauty. And although these may be
strengths-by-association, I will breathe deeply
of my own separate life before I slip away to
reunite with the source of all strength, light,
and permanence.

"I lie awake throughout the night, to meditate on your promise."
Psalm 119:148

42

DURING THE DAY a hundred noises and pressures come at us. The phone rings, the doorbell rings, the television drones. There are people to see, appointments to keep, work to do, children to care for. . . . We hardly have time to remember that the word *meditation* exists, much less time to meditate.

But in the quiet hours of the night, when the world is asleep and I am not quite, there is space and silence. In the night, I can hear the voice that is shouted down during the day, the voice of God, saying, *Peace, I am with you. . . . I will be your strength. . . . I will be your power. . . . I am the source of your life.* And like a silent night wind, blowing over the tiredness of my mind, I can feel power flowing into me, the steadiness that will keep me calm through a busy tomorrow.

*"He, Yahweh, is merciful,
tenderhearted, slow to anger, very
loving, and universally kind; Yahweh's
tenderness embraces all his
creatures."*
Psalm 145:8

43

IN THE WESTERN culture, we usually think of
God as the great Father of us all. But there
are some attributes of God that seem to be
more descriptive of a great mother. Mothers
are not logical creatures who hold their
children to the letter of the law. They are not
surprised when children are inconsistent,
irrational, peevish, or irritable. The mother
instinct makes allowances, avoids
punishment, tries to seal up the breaks in
relationships, forgets the rules, and always
reaches after the heart of the child in a kind
of searching, folding, flowing quietness.

Like a great mother, Yahweh embraces all
his creatures . . . the great Mother–Father.
This well-rounded love is the only power that
could ever turn the world into one family.

*"Not from the east, nor from the
west . . . but from God the judgment
comes, lowering one, raising another."*
Psalm 75:6–7

44

GOD IS THE judge. He lowers one and raises
another. On a very simple level we may take
this to mean that if we are "good" God will
reward us, or that if we please God he will
answer our prayers and do what we ask.

But there is a much more profound and
reliable meaning to these words. God is
central. He is the force that ultimately
triumphs over all the deviations and turns of
destructiveness in the process of life. And if
I am in the flow of that force, flowing with
God, my ways will be chosen, not because
they are mine, but because they are God's.
I am not bargaining with God to bend to my
will, but am joined to the power that cannot
lose.

*"Put your hope in Yahweh, be strong,
let your heart be bold, put your hope
in Yahweh."*
Psalm 27:14

45

HOWEVER WE EXPRESS it in many different
languages and concepts, there is only one
word in this world large enough to be our
ultimate hope; God.

If we reflect on past days, we will see that
every time there has been a deep
disappointment, a hurt, an alienation, it has
come when we ultimately hoped in a person,
an institution, a happening, or a desired
circumstance. Many times these fail to live up
to our expectations. But when our hope is
focused on the larger, the ever-powerful pure
creative love of God, following it without
demanding its direction, there is no deep
disaster that can touch us. We are anchored
in the Eternal.

*"Since you aspire to spiritual gifts,
concentrate on those which will grow
to benefit the community."*
1 Corinthians 14:12

46

MANY THINGS I can acquire in life are good,
but their acquisition stops with me. Even
abstract gifts such as enjoying a sunset or a
day by the sea or traveling to another
country. . . . These are gifts I take in. There is
no problem with taking in and enjoying life's
good gifts, but there arises in me the need to
give back, to distill the collection of what life
has given me and give it back to the world as
my own unique contribution.

If I can take every gift life brings me, cherish
it in my heart and mind, and then offer it
back to someone else, my life will not only
be for my private enjoyment, but will take a
constructive place in the human community.
As I choose my gifts of the spirit, let me select
those that will make good return gifts to the
world.

"I mean to praise Yahweh. . . . I mean to sing to my God. . . ."
Psalm 146:2

47

WE EXIST ONE STEP removed from joy because we spend our lives intending to be instead of being.

I mean to be a better husband or wife. I mean to be a better father or mother, or son or daughter. I mean to live by God's guidelines, to experience love and peace and power. I mean to, but . . . . But what?

The power of God within us can jerk us out of the torpid state of *meaning to be,* and lift us into the state of *being.* Starting today, I can *be* a better husband or wife. I will *be* a better father or mother, a better child or friend. I *will be*—no, I already *am* more joyous, because it is happening now. Love and peace and power are flowing through me. This is as I was meant to be. This is being-in-God.

"You must not do this."
Jeremiah 40:16

48

GEDALIAH WAS TOLD that he was going to be murdered, and was given a chance to strike his assassin first through the hand of his informer. But his words were, *"No, you must not do this."*

In the rough and tumble of living, I am sometimes given the choice to kill or be killed (not literally, of course, but in effect). Which should I do? Are my actions to be dictated by the violence of others, or am I to listen to the voice of God within saying . . . *You shall not kill. . . . You shall not steal. . . . You shall not bear false witness. . . .* But why not, God? Everybody does it, and it's the only way to survive. You just don't understand, God!

Then there drifts across my mind in a warm glow the image of one who made that different choice . . . to be killed rather than to kill. And having been willing to die, he is more alive today than ever. Strange how that turns out.

*"Yahweh, for at daybreak you listen
for my voice . . . at dawn I hold myself
in readiness for you."*
Psalm 5:3

49

EVERY MORNING WHEN I arise, full of the
confused dreams of the night, feeling the
demands of a new day, wanting good things
to happen or plans to come about, it is easy
to forget that my life needs a central
focus—a point around which it functions.

But there is a power waiting for me, waiting
to make contact with me, to energize me,
and send me out into the day with a sense of
wholeness and warmth and love. All I need
to do is to raise my spirit to receive that
contact, and I will feel a clearing of the
mind—will receive the power of God like a
new miracle, powerful enough for whatever
the day demands.

*"And forgive us our debts, as we have
forgiven those who are in debt to us."*
Matthew 6:12

IF ANYONE HAS offended me and it is more
than I can bear, let me look up at the cross
and remember that no matter how big that
wrong is, the meaning of the cross is bigger.

I do not have to bear the sins of the world. It
is God who forgives. If there is anything too
deep or too painful for me to forgive, let that
rest with God. It is too heavy for my
shoulders. In allowing God to forgive, I too
will be forgiven for claiming the responsibility
for what was not mine—another's
relationship with God.

Let me look up at the cross and breathe
deeply and smile. The offense is in good
hands. I am free.

"Wake up. . . . So far I have failed to notice anything in the way you live that my God could possibly call perfect."
Revelation 3:2

51

FAITH THAT TRIES to exist apart from a workable lifestyle is a dream—and not a very good one at that. In the world in which we live, people are looking for belief systems that work, loyalties powerful enough to affect and influence our values. A faith that goes doddering along on the side, mouthing platitudes, and chanting incantations will (rightly) be seen as a luxury few people can afford. But a faith that takes itself seriously enough to live what it believes will become a motivating force in a world that has lost its way.

The world is looking for leaders. Is it looking for the kind of faith I have?

*"When you go to the Temple, be on
your guard. Go near so you can
hear. . . . Be in no hurry to speak."*
Ecclesiastes 4:17–5:1

52

THE MORE ONE understands the mystery of
God's power in this world, the less one has
to say. A worship experience becomes a
clearing of the mind, a turning toward
openness and greatness. There is less to say
and more to hear.

And what is heard is not restricted to the
audible words spoken on a certain day. An
attitude of worship puts one's mind and spirit
in line with great wordless things; a flow of
power, a pull toward light, a surge of
strength. When these forces are felt, we fall
silent. What is there to say?

". . . you are my Son, the Beloved;
my favour rests on you. Immediately
afterwards the Spirit drove him out
into the wilderness and he . . . was
tempted by Satan."
Mark 1:11, 12

IN SOME MYSTERIOUS way creation and
destruction are closely intertwined forces, like
day and night. The more direct our contact is
with God the creator, the more keenly we are
aware of the destructive power in the world.

And this destructive power, this dark
element, calls to us. It whispers to us that if
we are the sons and daughters of God, why
not put on a big show, and turn stones to
bread, so the crowds will be convinced? And
if we are in God's care, why not prove it by
dangerous leaps from the temple? And if this
world is God's, why not prove it by
possessing as much of it as we can?

That subtle, subtle voice of darkness can only
be stilled when we answer that *God is,* and
he does not need us to prove it. Our attempts
to prove God only prove that we doubt him.

"Yahweh, now is the time to act."
Psalm 119:126

54

ONCE IN A WHILE I stroll out onto the stage of the universe, and give God his cue. *Now is the moment, God, step out and show what you can do. . . .* And every time I do this, I am struck, mid-gesture, with the foolishness of such a pose.

God is acting in the long, long drama of the ages, and I am not aware of the plot in its entirety. I may think it is time for God to act, when his script reads quite differently. There are millions of people in his cast of characters, all woven into a meaningful theme of creation and destruction and eventual triumph. Since I do not know when it is time for God to speak, it is wiser for me to stand in readiness, listening for the voice that will give me my small part of the action. It is only in quietly taking my part that I will begin to comprehend what the whole drama is about.

"The wound . . . wounds me too."
Jeremiah 8:21

55

So much of healing is in the mind. When I am burdened down and torn in spirit, my body is likely to break down. In order to heal the body, my spirit must also be healed.

And what is so healing as knowing that another person really cares? If I can look at someone who loves me, and know that he feels every pain I bear as though it were his own, somehow the pain is cut in half. And if I know that there is someone who truly wants me to be healed . . . someone who will also feel sick until I am whole, the incentive to be well will be doubled. The most terrifying aspect of being sick is being alone . . . of feeling that life is going on without me, and it does not matter. But when I realize I am not alone, that someone else really cares, I want to be well to share my health with the one who has shared my pain.

So much of healing is in the mind. By caring, we can all help to bring healing to each other.

*"How could we sing one of Yahweh's
songs in a pagan country?"*
Psalm 137:4

56

I HAVE BEEN A Christian all my life, yet I am
very sensitive about forcing my beliefs on
others. Perhaps I bend over backward in this
regard. I should learn to celebrate what I am.

Yesterday I met a boy I had known about ten
years ago. When I knew him his parents were
Buddhist, and he professed not to believe
anything. I had always been very careful not
to push him toward belief. But when I saw
him yesterday the first thing he said was,
"I'm a Christian now!" and there was a
bright light in his eyes. He was celebrating his
new found faith.

I keep remembering that sparkle in his
eyes. . . . I have been a follower of Christ for
a long time. Do I celebrate that faith,
wherever I am?

*"Physical exercises are useful enough,
but the usefulness of spirituality is
unlimited, since it holds out the reward
of life here and now and of the future
as well."*
1 Timothy 4:8

57

THE CULTIVATION OF insight is a useful and
exciting experience. So many of our activities
are hustle and bustle, with everyone busy
serving the cake and coffee or following the
agenda. But if we can train ourselves to sit
back and ask, "What is happening here?
What is being accomplished? What spirit
pervades this meeting? Are the people in this
place in touch with God? Am I? What can be
done to turn this gathering from a simple
cake-consuming party into a moment when
we all touch something vital?"

When we look back and remember life, the
vital spots will be those where we have
touched the eternal Spirit. . . . These
moments will be, as it were, our introduction
to the beyond.

"My soul is overcome with an incessant longing for your rulings."
Psalm 119:20

58

WHENEVER PEOPLE have a problem, they want to get together as a community or a family or a country to make a new ruling about it. If there were a rule, so the reasoning goes, it would be kept. But rules are not kept. It is laughingly said that rules are made to be broken. Once the rule is made, everyone feels the problem has been solved, and goes back to doing as he pleases . . . unless someone is looking.

Wanting rules and order . . . for the other person . . . is a deep instinct in us. But just as deep is the instinct of disorder, to do as we please. The only way these two warring factions in our nature can be united is to make what we *want* to do and what we *should* do one. This uniting process within us is called the love of God. It is shown in a love for people, and a love for the world. What I love I will not destroy . . . even when no one is looking.

"God's gift was not a spirit of timidity, but a spirit of power, and love, and self-control."
2 Timothy 1:7

59

EACH OF US IS IN charge of a complex life-operation. Power pours into us like raw electrical current, ready for us to put to use. Part of it is to be directed toward others in the form of caring, respect, support, and sharing. The rest is for our internal use—the spark that motivates our thoughts, ambitions, wishes, and drives.

Life-power is raw stuff and, if left unchanneled, can cause us internal damage and ruin everything around us. We need all the help we can get to take this power and shape it into a controlled expression of whole personhood. God has given us a spirit of power, but it is up to us to create out of it a mastered art-form of living.

"He wants everyone to be saved and reach full knowledge of the truth."
1 Timothy 2:5

THAT WORD "SAVED" takes a constant battering. People either simply believe in being saved, or they ask, "Saved from what?"

There are two things in this world that most human beings recognize we must be saved from. One is a sense of lostness, of being alienated from ourselves; and the other is a feeling of uselessness, of having no vital function which connects us with other people. The end of both of these is despair, and eventual self-destruction. But establishing contact with God gives us a sense of foundness, of knowing our own worth, of acceptance. It gives us the life-function of sharing the love of God with other people. It gives us hope, and makes us creative and vital. There's not only a lot to be saved *from,* there's a lot to be saved *for!*

*"In him there is wisdom, and power,
too. In him is strength, in him
resourcefulness."*
Job 12:13, 16

61

I DO NOT NEED much to get along in this
world . . . just a few simple things like
wisdom, power, strength and
resourcefulness!

If I had the wisdom to know what is right
amidst all the blur of choices I am given, and
if I had the power to live out that wisdom
when I *do* know what is right, if I had the
resources to meet life's emergencies and the
strength to carry on when not even an
emergency breaks the dull circle of
events . . . if I had all of these, I might begin
to know what it means to be a person
created in the likeness of God.

But I so quickly turn my back and go
thrashing around in the dark for insights,
answers, and resolutions, where none are to
be found. Why?

In God there is wisdom and power and
strength and resourcefulness.

"Be very careful about the sort of lives you lead, like intelligent and not like senseless people. This may be a wicked age, but your lives should redeem it."
Ephesians 4:15–16

LIVING WITH A sense of wholeness takes a great deal of thought. There are a thousand mindless patterns one can fall into, from senseless secularity to religious rigor. But a carefully lived life must take into account its origins, the fact that it stems from and is a gift of God, and then go on to enjoy every facet of that gift, delighting in the mind, the senses, the spirit.

But the Christian who tries to be well-integrated may be caught in the middle, equally misunderstood by those who have no standards and those who live by the rules. The world around us sneers at single-mindedness and honesty, and then pounces on those who are caught without them. The best way to be nothing is to try to be like everyone else.

Thank God, I do not have to be responsible for this whole world. In fact, if I succeed in living one well-integrated life, a minor miracle will have been accomplished—"redeeming" the age in a very small and personal way.

"Progress in the faith and even increase your joy in it. . . ."
Philippians 1:25

FAITH COMES TO people in many different ways. It may be a steady awareness of God from childhood on or a dramatic moment when one's life is changed. But however it comes, faith must keep growing in order to be the source of one's joy. A faith that stands still is dull.

But joy is like love or happiness or any other good thing. It eludes us if we go out and try to grab it by the tail. Joy comes to us the hard way, when we are thrown into difficult circumstances and our faith is put to the test. When we are absolutely at the end of our own resources and call on God to fill us with his power and wisdom to deal with a life crisis, we will know the joy that comes from renewed faith. And that strengthened faith must again be put to the test. A joy that is produced by constantly strengthened faith will never result in a faith that is dull.

"When Jeremiah had finished saying everything that Yahweh had ordered him to say . . . the priests and prophets . . . said, 'You shall die!'"
Jeremiah 26:8

IT IS A STRANGE situation when God's orders come and the priests and prophets contradict them. One would think that the professionals in religion would be those most in touch with the voice of God.

But this contradiction has existed ever since the worship of God has been practiced, and it certainly was present in the time of Christ. Religion seems to form its own protective crust, to ossify in its own routines, to justify its own injustices, and defend its own blindness. And when the prophetic word comes, called out from hearts attuned to a new drift of the Spirit, it can be the priests and prophets who feel most threatened.

Perhaps in the matter of being sensitive to God's voice, every priest and prophet must remain as open as if he were an ordinary man, and every ordinary man as if he were a priest or prophet.

"He who probes the inmost mind and the depths of the heart. . . ."
Psalm 64:6

WHY DO I WANT to do what I want to do? Is it to show off, to set myself apart, to impress people with what I have, or to be snobbish, relating to only those who I think will further my aims?

Or is it to follow a deep sense of adventure within, to do something together with people who need me, to get to know the value of interdependence, to store up enough love to last me for all of this life and well into the next one? No matter what we ask these questions about, it's not what we do, but why we do it that is important.

"What will you say when they descend on you as conquerors, those you yourself taught to be your friends?"
Jeremiah 13:21

THE MAKING OF friendships has a definite influence on one. What kind of friendships do I cultivate, and why?

There have been times when I thought it wise to cultivate friends who were different from me in every way, who challenged my ideas and ideals, who found my lifestyle charming and a little quaint. . . . Sometimes the reaching out to one's opposite can be refreshing, but at other times it can be destructive. When friendships force me to be what I am not, when the urge to conform robs me of my selfhood and leaves me empty, then I have been conquered by forces that can harm and disintegrate. It might be a good rule of thumb to make friends with those who would make good conquerors if they became stronger than I.

" 'So you have found me out, O my enemy!' 'I have found you out. For your double-dealing. . . .' "
1 Kings 21:20

67

OFTEN WHEN A disaster has come down on me, I can trace it to its origin . . . a point at which I thought I was being very clever, backing someone against a wall with a righteous smile on my face.

For a well-integrated and whole person, the best way to deal in life is straight-forward —never taking an unfair advantage, or doing the devil's work in the name of God. Disasters may still happen, even in the most well-ordered life; but if they do, they can be handled much better if they are honest accidents, and not coupled with the guilt of being something I have brought on my own head. Double-dealing closes in and strangles one in the end.

"May your good spirit guide me on to level ground."
Psalm 143:10

IT IS DIFFICULT to live a balanced life—one that is neither crushed beneath a feeling of hopelessness, nor inflated with too large a sense of self-importance. Of all the rainbow moods that filter across our consciousness during a day, how do we strike a self-concept that is healthy, real, integrated and whole?

There is a consciousness of the presence of God that can raise and lower me like a magnetic force. If I'm too low, the thought of that presence lifts me up. If I'm too high and mighty, the sense of that presence brings me down . . . there, on target, in center. The good spirit of God keeps me on level ground.

"'Stretch out your hand and lay a
finger on his possessions, and
I warrant you, he will curse you to
your face.'"
Job 1:11

IN THE STORY OF Job, there seems to be a strange negotiation going on. God is giving power to the evil one to hurt, but with restrictions. There is a struggle between the forces of good and evil for a man's soul, and yet one has the feeling that a subcontract is being let out to the devil for the accomplishment of God's purpose. It is a conglomerate we do not often think of!

How can something that cuts me, robs me, takes all that I have, and strips me to the bare soul be allowed by a God of love? It can be allowed in the same way that a demolition crew is part of a construction company. The end result is the creation of the new, but in the process, the old and familiar may be lost forever. To believe in God is to understand that the construction company hires the demolition crew, and it is never the other way around.

*"We have always treated
everybody . . . with the reverence and
sincerity which comes from God . . .
without ulterior motives."*
2 Corinthians 1:12

IT IS EASY FOR US to think of reverence and
sincerity as words which describe our attitude
toward God . . . but the flow can also run in
the opposite direction. Reverence and
sincerity are values which can flow *from* God
through us *to* other people.

In fact, the reverence and sincerity I owe
God can only be visibly expressed in my
relationships with those around me. But
I must remember that this reverence is
originally God's, and it cannot be used to
superficially "win friends and influence
people." It must be an honest encounter on
its own, letting the results fall where they will.
Giving to people the respect that we owe
God will not get us everywhere. It will only
get us the highest things in life.

". . . who turns rock into pool [and]
flint into fountain."
Psalm 114:8

71

WHEN WE LIVE with a consciousness of God
within us, there is a kind of magic about our
lives that we may not fully understand
ourselves. But it is understandable, if we
allow a little freewheeling between the
physical and the intangible worlds.

At the basis of creation, all matter is made of
the same elements. A stone and a stream
may appear to be opposites, but in the
interrelationship of things, they are akin. God
is the origin of natural law. From his wisdom
flow the chemical and physical changes that
convert matter from one substance to
another.

This creative power of God lives in me. If
I am willing to implement it in my life, I may
not be able to turn stones into water, but
I can learn to take hard, dry experiences
and turn them into living things . . . leaping
fountains of joy that spring from me and give
life and refreshment to all around.

"Yahweh, you bring strength to their hearts . . . so that earthborn man may strike fear no longer."
Psalm 10:17–18

72

THERE IS A WAY of living and achieving that seems very naïve to some . . . a longing for simplicity and beauty and a sense of human dignity that, even though it is too earthy for some, seems too heavenly for others.

For those who choose this way, the Christ-way, there is always the danger of being hurt—of suffering. When does one reach the sureness that this simple way is best? When is it impossible to be hurt by those who hold to more easily explained values?

When did Christ stop suffering?

"The sun rises, the sun sets. . . .
southward goes the wind, then turns
to the north. . . . what has been done
will be done again."
Ecclesiastes 1:4–5, 9

73

THE RHYTHMS OF the natural world can be
viewed two ways. One can see the constancy
of day and night, of sun and rain, of water
flowing to the sea and rising from the sea,
and be bored by it all, or one can see the
same processes and sense in them the
reassuring heartbeat of life.

I'm glad for the predictableness of day and
night, pleased by the centuries-long dance of
the world through the patterns of space. And
even though I will be here for only a
comparatively short number of years, I love
to think of a world that was here before I was
born, one that will go on dancing and
swaying to the drums of the universe after
my life has passed. Monotony? No,
continuity.

"He is the radiant light of God's glory and the perfect copy of his nature. . . ."
Hebrews 1:3

74

WHEN GOD MADE man in his own image, he must have become very tired of the dimness of the light that shone through man, and of the imperfection of that image which was cast in his likeness. Man could never quite reflect the glory he was meant to.

And then Christ came, a man in whom the light of God shone so brightly that the darkness shrank back in terror and schemed how to put it out, and the seekers of light came searching, wanting to touch the brightness they had always known they lacked. Before them was the kind of man they knew they were meant to be, the perfect version of their flawed natures: God's nature. And all who looked to him became a little brighter, a little more like God.

*"From east to west, praised be the
name of Yahweh!"*
Psalm 113:3

75

IN TIME AND SPACE, the Spirit of God knows no
limit. In traditions and cultures traces of this
spirit are found, but as soon as man tries to
define the essence of God, as soon as he
attempts to stylize and stereotype it, only
fossilized footsteps are to be found.

Even the usage of the English word "God"
restricts the image in our minds—restricts it
so that he must sometimes be left behind
with the archaic images we have formed. But
the essential presence of God is as boundless
as the sea, moving from the shores of the east
to the shores of the west, as flowing and
uncontainable as the clouds. Like the clouds,
God's spirit creates the atmosphere wherever
it goes, yet it is untamable, unpredictable,
unable to be caught or coerced to follow
man's patterns.

The great surging power of *Yahweh* be
praised from east to west!

*"I am happy, Yahweh, at what you
have done; at your achievements I
joyfully exclaim . . . immensely deep
are your thoughts."*
Psalm 92:4–5

76

SOMETIMES I FEEL I am only a piece of
driftwood, riding on the surface of the great
deep sea that is God.

Living a day at a time, dashing from one
place to another, sometimes wasting time . . .
I have only brief encounters with real
awareness. I do not always know what is
happening or why, or what effect it is having
on my life. I move in my pattern, back and
forth, toward shores that I have never seen. I
am conscious of movement, but what moves
me? Sometimes I do not even know, any
more than the driftwood on top of a great
wave knows. But I am happy, God, at what
you have done. Random as it has seemed in
the living, my life has been a great journey.
Your thoughts are the deep ones, God, and I
am grateful when, for a moment, I can touch
them.

"Proclaim his salvation day after day."
Psalm 96:2

ᄀᄀ
▬▬▬▬

Living a life in relationship with others, we will have conflicts . . . conflicts between parents and children, between friends and partners. One conflict is no sooner resolved than another seems to surface. The temptation is to throw up our hands and retreat into silent alienation. What is the use of problem solving if the supply of problems is endless?

At times like this, I look at the cross, and ask, *"Cross, what do you have to say to me? What difference does it make to be a Christian in these circumstances?"* And then the words come back, *"The difference it makes is that Christ is here."* Then I know that as each day's problems arise, I can meet them in the spirit of Jesus Christ, one who listened and loved, yet who had a core of strength. The salvation he brought was not only a once-in-a-lifetime thing, but a gift to be lived out day after day.

"Your commandments epitomise faithfulness."
Psalm 119:86

78

COMMANDMENTS SOUND like rigid, unliving things. Laws are cold, brittle, and unbending. Yet a society that is bound by laws is a stronger, more livable place than a lawless society. Why?

Artists know the laws of color. Blue is cold. Red is hot. Yellow is warm. Green is cool. Artists use these colors, knowing they are following established rules. To the beginning art student this may sound all wrong, and then, suddenly, there are shadows and spots of brilliant sunlight, effects the student artist would have found hard to attain by making it up as he went along. "Do it by faith," an art teacher once said. "Make your darks too dark and your brights too bright, and it will turn out too right."

Life . . . if I can *do it by faith,* I know that I will look back and marvel that I have done something so right, so livable.

"He is altogether lovable. Such is my Beloved, such is my friend."
Song of Songs 5:16

79

NO ONE CAN BE perfect every hour of the day. In a marriage relationship there will be moments of friction, times of hurt, or anger. But the strong bond that holds two people together through all the conflicts of everyday life is a broad and basic ability to see the other person as good, to see him or her as lovable, to be able to see all that the other person does through a screen of pre-concluded love.

Love, at its best, is a strong friendship—a friendship that not only respects and cares for and lifts up the other person, but one that has no bounds to the depths of expression. When a person is both lover and friend, that is the most profound relationship on earth.

"You are my son. Today I have become your father."
Psalm 2:7

ONE DAY WHEN THE bottom fell out of my life and I did not know which way to turn, I wondered what it meant to be a child of God—and suddenly without intending any disrespect to Jesus Christ the Son, I found myself praying a familiar creed.

I began in despair, affirming—I believe in God the Father almighty, maker of heaven and earth. . . . Yes, I can say that—and I believe in Jesus Christ . . . and I must believe in myself (name), as his son or daughter. My life came from God before it took on this human body. I live in a world where sorrow, injustice, and violence are common. But I believe the love of God will triumph. Sometimes it is not clear how right will win. I may be asked to go through hell, but I know I will have in me power to rise above it.

Yes, I believe in forgiving. I need other people. I know that as a Christian I share the responsibility of bringing to this world a sense of joy and beauty, and a quality of life that is everlasting.

*"Holy One, you make your home in
the praises of Israel."*
Psalm 22:3

81

THE PEOPLE WHO live each day with a song on
their lips and joy in their heart become God's
movable home.

Many times, during the history of Israel, the
people were taken into captivity. There was
no temple, no holy of holies, no priest or
any of the usual symbols of the divine
presence . . . and the people became sad and
lost. But once they began to sing their songs,
they reminded themselves of God. He came
alive and spoke to them through the words of
their own psalms. While they sang praises
they came to realize what Christ later put into
words . . . that the power of God does not
live in buildings made with hands, but within
the human heart. In the darkest, deepest
night of the spirit, a song can begin almost as
a cry of grief and end as a shout of triumph,
because in the singing of it we have
discovered that God is there, and that all will
be well.

*"You will have in you the strength,
based on his own glorious power,
never to give in, but to bear anything
joyfully."*
Colossians 1:11

TIMES OF STRESS, times of endless waiting, days of frantic work. . . . Sometimes we ask ourselves, do we have the strength to take any more of this? Can we face this?

The answer is always yes. We can and we will. Because of the power of God that lives in us, we are indestructible. We have the ability to never give in to despair, defeat, discouragement, dislike of others, the thirst for revenge, or any of the many destructive down-drafts that pull at our spirits. We have the power of God in us, ready to give us joy and peace and a strong sense of purpose. We can rise above this seductive sense of despair and see it for the trap that it is. We are filled with eternal life, and that is the longest-wearing substance in this world.

"Do not forget: thin sowing means thin reaping; the more you sow, the more you reap."
2 Corinthians 9:6

83

FEW THINGS IN life happen by accident, even though some events may come on us by surprise. For the most part our tomorrows are the result of our todays, and our todays are the result of our yesterdays.

Empty days, stretched toward some vague future when we expect some great happening, will only bring an empty future. People ignored or contacts unmade today will lead to lonely tomorrows. Work undone or relationships untended will lead to a feeling of isolation. Thin sowing means thin reaping. Perhaps the best way to live is to be so immersed in the sowing—the pure pleasure of plowing the field and scattering the seed—that the crop which results almost comes as a pleasant surprise . . . the feeling that life has been so full, how could there be this harvest on top of it?

"May my behavior be constant in keeping your statues."
Psalm 119:5

IT IS A COMMON concept in regard to our bodies that we are what we eat. In the same sense it may be said of the spirit that we are what we believe.

One time I met a man who was so calm, so steady, with such a reserve of strength that I wondered where he got it. And then, coming to know him better, I found that deep beneath the surface he had a heartfelt faith in God. He did not shout and wave it about, but it was there, molding his life. He believed that God is reliable, so he became reliable. He believed that God is just, so he became just. He knew that God is merciful, so he showed mercy in his dealings with others. God became the unconscious shape of his life, not something apart from his daily existence, but integrated into the very fibre of his character.

The truth is, We are what we believe—even if that is nothing.

"All I want is to know Christ and the power of his resurrection, and to share in his sufferings."
Philippians 3:10

THERE IS SOMETHING wistful and wonderful about the life and death of Christ that attracts like a magnet. I want to identify with it, to have that quality of wistful wondering within me. But there are elements of Christ's life, words like suffering and resurrection, that I shy away from. What could they mean to me?

Then it comes . . .

Almost imperceptibly it comes, the awareness of that *gap* between what I could be and am, and I know suffering. And when that suffering is magnified to a grand scale, when I sense the pain and lack of fulfillment in so many lives, physical death is not the greatest evil to be feared. What is important is to see the death of doubt and despair and hopelessness, and the resurgence of faith and hope and promise. To know the power of the resurrection is to have experienced it so many times that one knows nothing is ever the end, not even death.

"Seek Yahweh and his strength, seek his face untiringly."
Psalm 105:4

86

AS HUMAN BEINGS, we have a double need: to be fulfilled outside ourselves, and to be integrated within ourselves. It is the pull between these two needs that gives meaning and strength to life.

I may spend my life searching for a career on which to concentrate my energies, my ambitions, my talent, my need to achieve . . . and wake up someday to find that I am empty and hollow inside. Or, on the other hand, I may spend years cultivating my inner life, carrying on a private dialogue between my heart and my brain, and wake up someday to find out that nobody else cares. My life has nothing outside itself. How can I center on anything that will build me, both within and without?

God, the transcendent and the within, is the only point large enough to build a life on. Loving God teaches me to both reach for the stars and keep the home fires burning.

*"His peace can ransom me from the
war being waged on me."*
Psalm 55:18

87

LIFE IS CONFLICT. If we had a choice, few of us
would want it any other way. It is the process
of our inner selves reaching out and growing,
bumping against the environment, jostling
against the growing spirits of others. Conflict
is motion, is story, is plot and substance.
Where there is no conflict, people die
from lack of stimulation.

But in the middle of this life of conflict, what
can keep our heads steady, our nerves calm,
and give us a sense of balance? Perhaps it is
simply a quiet sense of God—of believing
that all, ultimately, will be right with the world
and, until it is, that God is there even in our
struggles. When the story of our life is
completed, it will be the conflicts we have
experienced that will have made it significant.

"You have shown your faith in action, worked for love and persevered through hope, in our Lord Jesus Christ."
1 Thessalonians 1:3

FAITH, HOPE, AND LOVE are the three great words of those who follow Jesus Christ. Although these are three distinct characteristics, they interact strongly with each other.

Faith gives us the insight to know what life is all about. It helps us see beneath the surface of what is, to the depths of what could be. Love gives us the power to live by faith's insights. It gives us the motivation to do things that would otherwise be totally impossible. . . . And hope gives us the courage to hang on even when we know that they *are* impossible. Hope leads us back to faith, to new insights, new love.

*"I know the trials you have had, and
how poor you are—though you are
rich—"*
Revelation 2:9

TRUE EVALUATION of a person's assets should
be registered on two different indexes. There
is the outer index, which is easily seen on a
balance sheet of assets and liabilities, and
although this may influence a person's peace
of mind, it can in no way measure the other
set of values, the inner index.

The inner index rises when the person
believes . . . believes in life, in God, in
himself or herself, and when a person is
inspired to contribute whatever is in his or
her power to make a difference in the world.
People rich in the inner index have a
sensitivity to beauty, to pain, to the whole
range of human emotions, so that no day is
ever the same. Simply being alive is a *rich*
experience.

*"Yahweh encircles his people now
and for always."*
Psalm 125:2

A CIRCLE IS COMPLETE, and never-ending. The
arms of people we love encircle us in a warm
embrace. Families are circles, taking us all on
a merry-go-round of joy and sorrow, love
and anger, despair and profound meaning.
The world is a circle, and every day it spins
around the sun, leaving us all a little dizzy
with war and peace, love and hate, want and
abundance. Life is a circle . . . we are born
with nothing, and we leave it all behind when
we go.

But the biggest circle of all is the love of God,
reaching around the whole span of his
universe, teaching us all in our joy and
sorrow, our laughter and pain what it is to
love, and how to love each other. The love
of God is our origin and our destination, our
final definition as human creatures who have
become whole.